A BELIEVER'S JOURNEY

VOLUME 1

DR. SORETTA PATTON

ISBN 978-1-0980-0521-4 (paperback)
ISBN 978-1-0980-0522-1 (digital)

Christian Faith Publishing, Inc.
832 Park Avenue
Meadville, PA 16335
www.christianfaithpublishing.com

Unless otherwise indicated, all Scripture quotations are from the King James Version of the Bible.

Printed in the United States of America

CONTENTS

Jesus, for your glory my story is told.
God, bring the memories that you desire
to be told by your grace to me.

My tongue is the pen of a ready writer.
—Psalm 45:1

CHAPTER 1

THE BEGINNING

When I was a child growing up on the southside of Chicago, I knew of love from my parents. We were in a family of five, I had four siblings, and we were a loving family. In growing up, we never talked about God, but we all loved the Lord. I don't remember being made to go to church because my parents, who were from the south, never required us to attend church. My father's mother believed in the Lord although I don't remember her taking us with her to church.

Growing up, I can remember some very interesting events that happened in my life. It was in the morning, I remember at the age of twelve turning thirteen, it was very important for me to get baptized. I remember it being one of the coldest days ever. It was bitter cold outside, and I had to walk about two and a half blocks in order to reach the church. I had to bring my swimsuit and cap. I prayed my hair would not get wet and that I wouldn't get sick. I remember praying, "Lord, please don't let me get sick."

Leaving my house was an adventure. I wore a jacket thinking that I would stay warm. I remember making it to the church and following the usher to the back of the church to prepare to be baptized. The pastor explained to the congregation the importance of being baptized at such a young age. I did not care about what the church thought, only how important it was for me to be covered by God and everything that went with being protected by God. The urgency to be baptized occurred when I was told that none of my actions, good or bad, would be recorded until I was thirteen years old.

It wasn't like I was disobedient or even mischievous in playing outside. I just worried about not being covered by Jesus. Once baptized, I was happy about being safe in God. I couldn't explain why it was such an urgency for my baptism to take place. I recall always being drawn to watch the movie *The Kings of Kings* on Thanksgiving and Christmas holidays. I never knew why I liked these movies, I just knew that when I watched them, I felt peaceful, and I knew I was being protected from what I did not know. The happiness in my family was devastated at the age of fifteen due to my sister being murdered by her husband. I didn't realize how the impact of her death would affect me.

I really couldn't understand why she had to leave in such a grotesque manner. Out of her union with her husband came my niece. It was mentioned that my niece was in the same location when her father shot and killed her mother, my sister. I thought I would never get over her not being there for me. She took me everywhere she went, and I know that we would have had a good time since I am older now. It was months I looked for her to come into the front door. God really had to get me through that moment.

When I was fourteen or so, I remember waking up in the morning, being fully awake but not able to move. I did not understand what was going on. I only knew that if I call on the name Jesus in my mind or be able to move just one finger, I would be able to come out of what was happening to me. I started out focusing on the name of Jesus. I repeated the name of Jesus several times. Somehow just repeating the name of Jesus in my mind, I knew this situation would change. I trusted that the Lord would deliver me out of the situation I was in.

Eventually I was able to move my finger, which broke the hold on me. I did not like being held against my will. I told my mother what happened to me. I asked my mom what had happened to me and why I wasn't able to move freely from my sleep. She allowed me to share everything about the event with her. My mom did tell me it was some type of spirit. Lying there, I kept thinking that if I just could move my finger or toe or even open my mouth, I would be able to break this hold on me. I did not know what was happening to me. It was quite frightening.

Days past and I found myself thinking about what had happened to me. I now know, I just have to begin to say to myself, *Say the name of Jesus* over and over, if it were to happen again. Within minutes I was able to move my finger. I went to my mother again and asked her what was going on and why I could not move. My mother told me of a story when, as a little girl, where she and her sisters, while sleeping in their room, would hear something jump off of the dresser and then the light would come on.

Then she said it was some type of spirit. I was more afraid then of my mother's stories because I was a little girl experiencing these spiritual events. My mother's understanding was not enough for me to be confident in protecting myself from any more of these events. This event has never repeated itself. I wondered what it must have been like to hear something jump off the dresser and cut the light in the room on. To hear something move and thump and not see it when it cut on the light must have had my mother and siblings really scared. This must have been an important event because my mother remembered to tell us about it.

I also remembered being a little bit older and being awakened by some unseen spirit tapping me on my forehead between my eyes. Without opening my eyes, the tapping would stop when I became conscious to the tapping of the finger on my forehead.

I never asked my mother about this event because I did not feel constrained in anyway. I was not afraid. I never thought about this event anymore. This event never happened again, and I did not feel fear. I always felt that an angel was watching over me. I can remember lying in bed when my parents weren't at home and could feel a small dog walking between my legs. I would hate being at home alone when I had to be in bed at a certain time for school. Many times my mother would tell us who lived in the house before us. My mom would say that there was an old couple that lived in this house before us, and they had a dog. The community was set apart as a luxury complex for whites only in the 1950s and 1960s. The pictures that my mom showed us were of manicured trees and well-dressed lawns.

The neighborhood grew in families not like those before who cared for their homes. The transition went from manicured trees and lawns to run-down areas where trees did not exist. The stories also went from interesting stories of the many families that lived in the neighborhood to who knew who or so and so was caught in a gang fight. I know now that it was God's grace that kept us safe from the horrors that could have befallen us. There were times fear was around every corner, and just to go the local grocery store would be a challenge.

My mom worked at the community center as we grew older. We were beginning high school. She would call us to come and walk home with her. My brother and I would take off running to the community center to meet her. I was so glad to see my mom. My brother was also happy to see her as well. We both had faith in God that He would always protect us and keep us safe.

As my mother and father aged, we were always grateful for being together. My mother was the first person in her family to graduate with a bachelor's degree. My father wanted to follow her lead in school but could not because he worked. He still shared in her joy. From this special event, all of my siblings graduated from high school during a time where school could have been skipped due to noninterest and life's journey. My mother and father saw all of their children complete high school and some, even college.

My mom knew she was the foundation. She opened doors to the awareness of education for all of her legacy. This was the motivator for us to complete high school as well as go on the college in diverse areas of education. I know that my parents would be proud of what has been achieved from their offspring. My parents expired within two to three years of each other. My mom missed my dad—something fierce. She could not burden not being with my dad. They were married thirty-seven years and never spent more than a day apart. Sometimes, I think of them when I would achieve a goal in my life. My children kept my mother busy when my father expired.

I was told that he had given his life to God before his health turned for the worst.

I was very happy that my dad had given his life to Christ before he transitioned. I thought our family was special in that we grew up with my mother having a little time to share her experiences she had as a youth.

CHAPTER 2

FAMILY

My mother began to tell me of demons that rob people of their freedom to move at will. She called them evil spirits. I asked why did they choose me. She said she did not know, but it had happened to her when she too was a little girl. The conversation never went further than that. I had my answer and was determined to pray every night before I went to sleep to combat being attacked while sleeping.

None of my siblings ever mentioned having an encounter like the one I had. I knew our family was special because of the conversations that I would overhear.

I knew both of my sisters were special. They would sometimes talk about what was happening to them as they experienced the supernatural. My mother was very special; she had an identical twin sister that when we visited, they fooled us by pretending to be the other sister. I remember my aunt being left with us while my mom and dad would go off to visit other members of my mother's family. We never cried because we thought our mom was right there with us even though it was her twin sister, my aunt.

This would also happen when my cousin, who lived in the same state, would have errands to run and needed my mom, her aunt, to keep her kids. My cousin's children never cried either because they thought my mom was their grandma.

We would have a great time and would be very much so surprised to see mom and dad entering in the front door from visiting with my mother's other family members. We would look at each other in amazement because they looked so much alike.

My mom and her sister even had the same items in their homes. This amazed me because of the similarities in style and in color schemes. For example, my mom had a certain clock on the wall and my aunt had that exact same clock on her wall! I remember my mother was sitting on the couch, and suddenly she said, "I feel a sharp pain in my chest."

I immediately went to her to see if I needed to call 911. She said, "Oh, I am all right. My sister is having surgery, and I just felt the knife as they were cutting her." Of course my mouth was wide open in astonishment because my aunt lived in another state. There were many incidents that alerted me to my mother's ability to call out insightful information that no one could have known but the Lord.

My mother's father and uncle were Indians although they did not live on a reservation I think. My grandparents had a lot of land. I am not sure of how many acres. My grandmother was so light skinned with very long straight hair that I sometimes thought she was white, European, but that could not be true because my mother would have to be white, and I knew that was not true because my father was African American.

My grandmother was very nice and kind and could cook like nobody's business. When she did cook, the food would be so good that after eating, my brother and I would sit on the porch all day until dinner. Breakfast was at 6:00 am. We did chores every day. Our chores consisted of picking peas and butter beans. Bees were attracted to the flowers of the peas, and butter beans were huge. They never bothered my brother and I while we were picking peas or butter beans.

My mother and my aunts did all the cooking when we went to visit. We would travel down south a lot during warmer months. My grandfather, my mother's father, was a to-the-point type of person when in a conversation with the men of the family, and that included my father when we would visit. He was a man of few words. He was always observing the other family members when they would come by. I guess he wanted to join in the conversation. My grandfather was a very nice and kind man.

As I grew up, my grandparents expired almost at the same time. We only went down south to visit my aunt who was the caretaker of my grandparents every now and then before she expired.

My mother told us that we were from the Blackfoot Indian tribe. I was so excited to know that I was connected to a people who were here and survived all of the plights that were presented to them. I found out that my grandfather had a brother. I never knew this when I was a child. My mother rarely discussed her childhood with us. Maybe because we did not ask her about her childhood; this was a big mistake on our part. I think about the many questions I could have asked my aunt about their childhood.

I have found out through another aunt that my second cousins on my mother's side were alive. My second cousins, my mother's first cousins, were still alive; this meant that my grandfather's brother's children were still alive. I got very excited. My aunt shared stories about my granddaddy taking them to see their grandma, my great grandma, in horse and buggy. My aunt said she was six or seven years old when my granddaddy would take them to see his mother. My aunt said that my great-grandma was from the Blackfoot Indian tribe.

My great-grandma's name was Minnie, and she had extremely long straight black hair that reached down her back to her hind parts. Great Grandma Minnie was very dark skinned. I thought her description was of a very strong and beautiful woman of color. My great-great-grandfather was a Blackfoot Indian. My great cousin told me that my great-great-granddaddy had thirteen children! How exciting! I plan to visit my cousins a lot and learn more about my Indian side of the family. I think the odds are great that more of great-grandma's siblings had children, and I am hopeful I can trace my Indian heritage and learn more.

God is awesome to bring this revelation news to me. I am so grateful of Jesus to open this door for such a time like this. Being the youngest girl in my family, I did not know a lot of my family's history. I am, however, making a change in my life to building a relationship with the family I now know of. I am now in the process of connecting with my great uncle's children to learn more about my family, heritage, and legacy. I can only imagine the great stories that await me.

My brother was so excited when I shared this information with him. He also longed to hear the news of our Indian heritage. We both realized that someone had to pray for us since we both have spiritual gifts and a deep love relationship with our Lord Jesus Christ.

The land my grandparents owned was very old and most likely had stories to be told. When we visited my grandparents' house, my mother would tell us stories that were phenomenal because they involved supernatural or spiritual occurrences.

I remember being told stories of different animals that would come close to the house because the deep forest areas encircled my grandparents' house.

I also remember looking out of the bedroom window feeling like something was looking at me. I never had any spiritual experiences while in the company of my family. My grandparents in the early years moved to the northern states to be closer to their children. What made traveling so special is that when it was time for bed my mother would tell my brother and I of her spiritual occurrences.

My mother would tell us how she and her brother and sisters would come from church, taking the quickest route, which took them through familiar dark places that contained a grave site they past going to church. She told us of how they would see light shadows at the grave site, and they would run all the way home.

I opened with this story to give sight into the way I grew up. My mother was the one who instructed us, her children, in the way of spiritual gifts. She would have dreams about the future of occurrences.

I know that all of my aunts and uncles had special gifts as well. Photos of my uncles and aunts revealed that all of them were fair skinned and had either wavy or straight jet-black hair. My aunts and uncles also had unusual eye color. Some of my aunts and uncles, including my mom, had gray, green, and even hazel eye color.

With that being said, I can only guess that each of them could go into the spiritual realm. My thinking on spiritual gifts are based on my mother being gifted; therefore, her siblings also had to be gifted. My great-great-grandma, even my great grandmother, Minnie, must have had prayed for her great, great, great grandchildren because both my brother and I have spiritual gifts from God, as well as our mom being able to know about events and see visions.

For example, we would be at home playing a family game, and Mom would close her eyes and tell us the numbers that would be fluorescent to her. Mom would tell us what she had seen. More often than not, she would be correct.

I never played the numbers in the lottery, but my siblings did and would win. It was amazing to see my brothers and sisters come back home with their winnings. My mom could not explain why she had these abilities. She only knew she wasn't the only one of her family that possessed this talent. Maybe my great-grandma had these talents as well. I would think about the many questions I would ask my great-grandma Minnie. Questions like: Did she have spiritual gifts? What role in the Blackfoot community did great-great-grand-daddy play? Were they Christian?

I noticed that family members were expiring frequently. I did not understand why my family members were dying off at a certain age. I was confused. I began to reach out to God more at the age of seventeen. I remember being afraid after graduating from high school in three years. I had to believe that God has us all in His hands. It wasn't until my family members started to expire at sixty-two years of age. Clearly this was not what God says in His Word. Genesis 6:3 (KJV) which promises 120 years of life.

Trusting took on a new meaning for me to trust God. My brother took a different route in developing an intimate relationship with God. My life, however, took a turn for the better when I realized I needed God to lead and guide me in life. Many things happened which made me think someone was trying to hurt, harm, and create havoc in my life. Trusting did not come easy, neither did letting *control* go and trusting God.

CHAPTER 3

TRUSTING GOD

I was married and had a son. I was clueless as to what to do next. God put on my heart: remember Matthew 6:33: "*Seek ye first the Kingdom of God and his righteousness and all these things will be added to you.*"

My mother-in-law began to talk to me about Jesus. My mother-in-law told how Jesus would protect me and keep me safe. She told me that I only had to believe that God would protect me. She also shared with me that the love of God was greater than any other love. My husband and I got divorced at that point, I had to come up with a plan of how to make it in this world with a child. Heartbroken and feeling betrayed, I knew that God would take care of us. As time moved on, I thought we would reconcile our marriage. My husband joined the military in an attempt to get out of his obligations.

The only good thing that came from that attempt was another child—a beautiful baby girl. I knew I was having a girl because I saw her in a dream. I told my mother-in-law that I was not going to name her. My mother-in-law said, "What do you mean? You are not going to name the baby?" I told her that I believed that God would name her, so I didn't give her a name. I was seven months pregnant and did not realize that I had brought a pink beach ball in celebration of my baby girl coming into the world soon.

I remember picking up the beach ball and writing Naharia on the ball. I looked at the name: "*Naharia*" and thought, *Wow, what a beautiful name.*

In 1 Chronicles 11:39, it mentions *Naharai as the berothite*, the armor-bearer of Joab, the son of Zeruiah. Berothite means "well."

Wells run deep however, and most contain water, a substance by which sustains life. Jesus is the way, the truth, and the life. God sustained Moses with living water and the bread of life.

My daughter was born however I suffered a setback and began to bleed horribly. I had a C-section, and something must have gone wrong. I was told not to lift anything or do any excessive walking. I, of course, wanted to clean my house and moved furniture, I pushed the couch. I went to my mother's house and tried to relax. At around 1:00 a.m. I went to the bathroom and could not get up. I was bleeding so bad my mother began to talk to me, calling my name repetitively. I told my mom to keep calling my name. I knew if she didn't, I wouldn't have written this book. Nothing like this happened when I had my son, Raimondi.

I remember that when I went into the hospital, I was afraid when I had my son. My husband and parents took me to the hospital. The nurses prepped me for delivery they put me in a room all by myself and cut the lights off. I remember calling out to Jesus, asking Him not to leave me because I was so afraid. I reached out my hand, and felt another hand grab mine and squeeze my hand back. I was taken by surprise and released my grip and knew at that moment the Lord was with me. I thought about that time in the hospital when I was having my son and how Jesus was with me then I knew, He would be with me now in this life-threatening situation.

For some reason, I started out not afraid until my mind was telling my body to get up, but my body would not respond. Throughout that day, I had to wear a towel in order to catch the blood that was passing from my body. Blood began to clot and got to the size of a baseball. I prayed, "Lord, save my life. You gave me a baby boy and now a baby girl. Don't let me leave them."

My mother insisted that I stay with her until I got better. I was happy to know I would recover in my parent's home. My doctor did an emergency procedure which removed the pressure that caused the bleeding. After about three months, I was fine and returned home from staying at my mother's house. I needed her help, and she was happy to give it to me. Every day that I stayed with my mother, I was grateful that God spared me to be in this world to see my son and daughter grow. My daughter grew up strong and determined to be her best; she joined the military right out of high school.

My daughter, Naharia, has always had a passion to take care of people. She entered the military at a young age, and continued to grow in leadership while earning a position and degree which allowed her to assist those who needed help while in the military. She too has gifts from God and her faith, belief, and trust in God is phenomenal. Her brother, Raimondi, has been a huge influence on her life. My son, Raimondi, also has a passion for helping people. As a child, he had lung issues which he grew out of. Raimondi is a registered nurse and works in the emergency room. When we get a chance to talk, we get deep into the work and word of God. I enjoy the conversations we have.

My kids grew, and my love grew for Jesus after I let Him have my marriage. I began to establish a relationship with the Lord. I remember writing love letters to Jesus. I filled a spiral notebook with "I love you, Jesus." I wrote this over and over again in gratitude for the love and kindness Jesus had shown me. From that point in my life, I knew something had changed me. My husband and I parted ways, and there were no hard feelings.

I chose to let Jesus handle that situation. I was not sure how to raise two children, so I turned to the Bible. I remember reading in the books of Samuel and the story of Hannah and how she made a promise to give her son back to God if he blessed her. I committed my son and daughter to God because I knew that Jesus would keep them safe.

I knew that when they grew up and had hard decisions to make, God would be there. I knew I would not be able to surrender answers to questions they may have regarding life, issues, and circumstances. I trusted God to be there and provide whatever my children needed to keep them in His way, as well as protect them. The devil could not have them. I cannot share enough, how many times I have called on God, and He has been there to secure them in their time of need. I got married again years later. I had a son and named him Dwayne Matthew after my granddaddy. My baby boy, Matthew, is very special that God blessed his comings and goings. Matthew has encountered other incidents that tried to take his life. I began to wonder what was going on with Matthew, that he was being attacked by the devil.

This event that happened to Matthew caused the Holy Spirit to give me a dream that scared me intensely. In my dream, my son had a new sky blue car that my ex-husband had brought him to get back and forth to school. I could not see an accident. I just knew in my heart that I would never see Matthew again. In my heart, I was very sad. My son was alive but dead at the same time. I knew that the car was the reason why he lost his liberty. I told Matthew's dad my dream, and he agreed with me to get rid of the car.

It so happened that the car was very clean and in good condition (no dents). Around that time my son was trying to get into a relationship with a young lady whose morals were less desirable by anyone she had a relationship with.

It seemed as though Matthew did not have a hold on his thinking and emotions. One day, Matthew called me and told me he had to take his car to his dad to get some repairs. This was a different car. I asked him what was wrong with his car, and he told me that he could not stop the car, and by grace, it ran out of gas. Later, Matthew told me that the repairman working on his car asked him if he was a likable guy. My son told me the repairman said that someone cut his brake line and it was a miracle that he was not in an accident. I asked Matthew where he was trying to get to, and he replied he went to the girl's house he was trying to date.

It seemed to me that the young lady was working for the enemy. Every time Matthew tried to treat the girl like a young lady, she in response would do something that would disgrace him.

One night, I received a call from Matthew. His voice sounded troubled. I asked him what was going on. Matthew said the girl he had been seeing kept sending mixed messages, and she was not true to their relationship.

He sounded as though he was at his last end. The fear of him doing something to harm himself came into my mind. I began to tell him that if he did something to himself or bring harm to his life, the devil would have won. I told my son that there was greatness inside of him and he belonged to God alone. I trusted God to keep Matthew safe from her. I also had to tell him that if he killed himself over a girl that would not matter in six months, all his father and I could do would be to cry and bury him.

I reminded him that I gave him back to God in the womb as Hannah did when God opened her womb. She gave God her son, Prophet Samuel, which she promised to give back to God (I Samuel 1:28, KJV).

I got a text from the girl. I told her that my son's soul belonged to God, and she replied, "I will bury you and have your grandkids!" I told her my son belonged to God. That was when Matthew had just got out of high school and was planning to go to college. Shortly, after that I told Matthew that he was special to God as all of his sisters and brother were. I shared that his gifts from God came with authority that God trusted him with. I am grateful God intervened and gave him sense to realize that she would not even be in his life. Matthew forgot about that girl after He filled his life with other wonderful young ladies.

Trusting God in every area of my life is still ongoing. My baby girl, Nikki, was named after me. I named my daughter after me because of the uniqueness of why my mother named me as she did. My mother and her sisters must have played a game while having kids. I have several cousins with "etta" being the last sequence in their name. For example: Charlesetta and Rosetta were my cousins, and Loretta was my sister.

Nikki, however, is short for Monique. Birthing a baby named after you is kind of special. It marked the end of my baby having days as well as providing memories up to that special moment that I looked into her face. Nikki was born on my father's birthday and named after me. The way I chose to commemorate my father's love was by having her on his birthday. I am so satisfied with her that she sometimes has his grin and smile. She also has gifts from God, and yes, I gave her back to God just as Hannah did with her son, the prophet Samuel.

She is brave, smart, and fearless like her older sister. I have no idea where they got their fearlessness from if it had not been for Jesus Christ. As Nikki grew up, she graduated from high school and went to stay with her sister to attend college. Her sister was stationed in Hawaii, so Nikki attended Hawaii Pacific University (HPU). Her braveness was displayed when she called me and said, "Mom, I want to go to Howard University." Bravery took hold of Nikki when she got on a plane from Hawaii and flew home and then to Howard University and accomplished what could only happen in two to three months in one weekend.

Nikki got her school schedule, financial aid, and a place to stay in three days! Then she flew home and stayed a couple of days then back to her sister's house in Hawaii to close her accounts. I was amazed at how the hand of God moved in her life. There are more amazing events Nikki experienced while on her college journey. Most times, when being led by God, my children shared they knew it was going to happen because they asked God for it. I have told my children that they belonged to God. I shared with my children how I gave them back to God and that they belonged to Him and no harm or danger would befall them because God had destined their lives to glorify Him.

CHAPTER 4

BELIEVING IN GOD

I had one sister that was murdered by her husband that left our family empty. My other sister had heart surgery and was given a heart that was not working for her. That heart stopped on her many times. I remember not allowing her to drive herself to the hospital, and as soon as we made it to the hospital, she was rushed into the emergency room. A nurse came out to ask if I was her family, and I indicated I was her sister. I am gathering that her heart had stopped, and they were working on her. The result of the visit was that she needed a defibrillator to keep her heart going. She had been the guest on many television shows that the discussion topic was dying and coming back.

She later expired due to the heart that she received was not the one she was supposed to receive so it was not compatible with her body. She also loved the Lord, immensely. As family members would expire, it became very difficult to understand why. I really didn't understand why so many were taken away from my family (me) so fast. As I began to depend on God, I wondered if I was the cause of their early departure from earth. My father was the next to depart this earth. He was a kind and protective man who got saved late in life because he wasn't required to go to church. I am very happy my dad completed his life with the Lord Jesus being part of it.

Moving forward, the Lord provided information on how to achieve closeness in Him, I realized I wanted to give my all to order to receive from Him what He had promised me in the Bible.

Shortly, after I got married, I gave my life to God and was saved. I read the Bible and all of the amazing stories. I began to want what God had promised to those who believed in who He said He was. I wrote love letters to Jesus.

I repeated over and over again: "I love you, Jesus." I filled a notebook with those four words that shaped my life. Jesus remembered my words and has always protected me. I realized that I could trust the Lord. Whenever life took a turn for the worse or whenever I needed someone to talk to, the Lord always would reveal His presence to me.

When I drew close to Him, He drew close to me. Taking what I had learned in life allowed me to seek His face. When I was in high school, I recall I had the ability to call individuals in the air and they would get in contact with me. I remember choosing the Lord, His life, and His everlasting grace and mercy. I chose to trust the word of God even though I knew that I was reaching further into the spiritual arena. I knew things that would be true. I remember I called my sister (when she was alive) and told her what I heard in the spirit. She called the company, and they verified that there was a flight with that number going in the direction that I had indicated.

My niece and nephew could hear my sister reciting what I had shared with her over her conversation with the company. They called me and asked me what was given to me, and I indicated what I knew. They indicated that all of the individuals with the eye of sight were in their registry and they were not notified of any problems. I said okay and left the situation alone. Well, something did happen to that scheduled flight, and my sister was amazed at what I told her I heard.

I had made up my mind that I did not want to know events that did not come from the Lord nor did I accept being labeled anything less than a child of the Most High God. I trust God, and I have copied God's servant James in saying, "I am the servant whom Jesus loves."

I made the choice to give my children back to Him as Hannah did with her son, Prophet Samuel, I knew that I made the right decision because of how the prophet was taken care of being in the hands of God. I trusted Jesus to keep my children and family safe from all hurt, harm, or danger. To be a young African American woman raising four kids alone meant that I was naive about relationships, life, and raising kids. I knew that if God did it for Hannah, He would do it for me. I needed Jesus to protect my kids when I wasn't around or when they had to make decisions about matters that I did not have answers for.

One morning I was called to praise God in my basement. I did not know what was going on. I only knew that I had to worship until I was guided to stop. After about a half hour, my phone rang. It was my son, Matthew, saying that a car had went through the stop sign, where they were stopped at and hit them. I went right away to where my son said the accident was. When I arrived, my son and everyone in the car were walking around looking at the car.

Apparently, a car ran through the stop sign and hit them so hard that the car my son was riding in was wrapped around the light post. They were safe without injury. Both airbags had deployed, and no one was hurt. All I could do was praise and thank God for the grace He had shown to my son and his friends. There were several incidents that involved my son where God protected him.

Matthew was born on the fourth of July. He is a mild-mannered man with morals and values centered on Jesus. I am careful not to take credit for the work that God has done in his life. He is strong in the Lord like all my other children.

One morning, I received a call, about five years ago, from one of my son's friends telling me that my son was in a motorcycle accident and he was in the hospital. My daughter said that she would go, she went to the hospital. When she arrived at the hospital, she entered Matthew's room and made sure that her brother was well taken care of. She said she found in my son's hospital room a vial of blood left on the counter. She brought the vial home. She told me how she remembered when she was with her first child how close I stayed with her.

After she gave her son back to God in her womb, she knew that He would take care of him. Well, when she was having Braxton Hicks contractions or false labor pains, we went to the hospital, and that is where I found a vial of blood left on the counter in the room she was in. I remember sharing with her a book that I read about a woman of God who helped a young lady who had been given to the devil from birth because her mother was unwedded.

I shared that the book indicated that the devil gains control of young kids through unwedded mothers who come into the hospital for some reason or the other for treatment. A witch would pose as an employee of the hospital and in a position as a phlebotomist would take blood of the mother and in the basement of the hospital perform evil acts over the unborn child.

But when the child is given back to God as Hannah gave the prophet Samuel, the unborn baby is protected and no harm can come to the unborn baby because of the Blood of Jesus! The blood is so powerful that no evil can befall the unborn child.

The vial of blood was of no use to the devil because both mother and child belonged to God. So my daughter brought the vial of blood home that she found on the counter in my son's hospital room. He too was given back to God in the womb! (John 6:3, 45, 51 KJV)

The mistake was in thinking that an African American male was probably born to an unwed mother and she was in some kind of unfavorable situation. My son sustained lacerations to his leg when he tried to turn at the last minute into a curve lane under a viaduct. He had to have surgery to his leg. Skin was grafted from his upper thigh on to his leg. His little finger had the nail digit slightly removed as it healed. When my daughter brought him home, the Holy Ghost began to tell me what had happened to him. The devil wanted to kill my son, plain and simple.

Matthew made the turn on the curve of the road, and his motorcycle delayed in its lane to follow the road. The Holy Ghost showed me that two huge angels of God that are assigned to Matthew bowed the entire concrete wall that would have taken Matthew's life. It was a split second in time, but it was the only way Matthew survived the event. Matthew listened to me tell him of the accident, he began to cry. He said it was exactly the way the Holy Ghost told me it happened. God's grace and mercy truly protected him.

God assigned His most powerful angels to be there for Matthew when he needed them. God is awesome! In the back of my mind, I keep thinking that Matthew has a greater calling on his life, and the Lord is playing it out in him, slowly but surely. I feel that my son has a ministry calling for the word of God on his life.

When Matthew was in the hospital, he was given the same thought that every young African American male would have been given.

Matthew was not from a fatherless home. Note the fact my husband and I were very happy in our marriage before outside factors governed the outcome of our soon-ended marriage. God knows how to keep His family happy.

CHAPTER 5

VISIONS

When I started seeing visions in my mind or events of a person's future, I wondered if I could trust what I saw. I heard a prominent preacher's wife say that when she got saved, she asked God to do something with her life. All that I had known about Jesus and all He had done for me and my family, I knew I could trust Him. I asked God, the God that I trusted, to do something with my life. I wanted more of Him. I know Jesus protects me, and my faith is in Jesus. The Holy Ghost has taught me what I needed to have in my life and what changes were needed in areas of my life I had to lose.

I know that from a young age, I had experienced spiritual events. I would be at home in the bed waiting for my mom and dad to come home. Sleeping in my bed, I would feel small feet walking in and out of my legs. I would then see in a vision a small dog walking in and out of my legs. When I asked my mother about a dog being in the house, she told me of a white small dog that resided in this house that expired before we moved in. This event happened maybe once more then stopped.

Most of the time when I experience spiritual events, I was ignorant to what was happening. I asked Jesus for the truth. I wrote letters to Jesus expressing my love for the Lord because of the kindness and protection He had provided to my family. I was never afraid of the unseen.

Visiting my daughter in Hawaii, I was listening to the word of God. The preacher said, "Why would you invite something into your house if you cannot see it?"

I shared this with my daughter and her friend, the doorbell rang, but no one was there. I said, "In the name of Jesus, leave and never return." The doorbell never rang again. This happened on one more occasion in a different location. I was sitting at a friend's house, and the doorbell rang. Matthew went to the door and looked out to see who had rang the doorbell. I asked Matthew, "Who was at the door?"

He replied, "No one." I told him to never open the door when there is no one there. I told Matthew to say, "In the name of Jesus, leave and never return." He said what I told him.

I gave that concern to Jesus and never thought about it again. Before my husband and I separated, he was a witness to one of the supernatural events that happened in my life. I was at home walking on my treadmill, from out of nowhere, I knew something was wrong. I continued to walk on my treadmill. I just knew that a child was going to expire. I told my husband of what just came to me. I asked Jesus, "Please don't let it be one of mine." My husband answered the phone because I had decided to lie down until I had clarity on what was revealed to me. He brought the phone to me, and my niece's mother was on the phone telling me that my great nephew had expired because his navel cord had not healed. My husband had not seen anything like that before. He witnessed the power of Holy Spirit.

I fasted a lot during those days. I did not know what else to do. I learned, from reading the Bible, it would draw me closer to Jesus. My niece began to trust God in this area of understanding and why her son (gift) was released from life. She now has two children and is a better steward over the children (gifts) God has given to her.

One day, I tried to define my spiritual gifts. I prayed, and the Holy Spirit brought understanding to me that if I had not released my life to Jesus, the devil would have deceived me into thinking my gifts were from him. I am grateful for the Lord Jesus never letting me go (John 10:28, KJV). In the Bible, John 10:28 says, "And I give unto them eternal life, and they shall never perish, neither shall any man pluck them out of my hand." I have been told how strong in the spirit I was. I was told that I reside in the third heaven with Jesus and God Almighty. I only knew Jesus was protecting us.

When I went to church I felt at home. My soul was so satisfied there was a comfort and peace I would feel every time I was in church. Reading the Bible is key in obtaining the word, it will change the way things appear in your life. I have lived with gifts, the enemy tried to confuse me with knowing my power and authority is in Christ Jesus. I was in training in another location away from my home where I had to leave for weeks at a time, I was allowed to come home on the weekend.

I had a dream so real that my heart ached in the dream. I had dreamed that my mother had passed away. I jumped up and called her, and she answered "Hello" in the most kind and warm voice I ever heard. When she answered the phone and I heard her voice, I was so happy however, in a matter of two weeks, I received a call from my cousin, who had been staying with her, that she had expired.

My niece was sleeping in her bed, and she said, "Grandma woke me up to get her some water, and I found her on the couch. She looked as though she was asleep." My cousin said that my mom's legs were ice cold; that's how he knew she had expired. I had to give all my family who had expired to Jesus to keep safe so no door or gateway could be established that would distract me. I knew that they were a part of the cloud of witnesses cheering me on down here on earth (Hebrews 12:1, KJV).

When I read the Bible where Jesus responded, "Let the dead bury their dead" (Luke 9:60, KJV), I understood that to mean let those who did not know of Jesus are as dead, so allow them to bury the dead. I prayed, believing James 5:16 (KJV): "The effectual fervent prayer of a righteous man availeth much." I knew because of James 5:16, Jesus heard my prayers. I wanted God to trust me with the authority and power He had given me. My faith had to grow, and I knew if I asked for more of Him, I would receive it.

Now that my family was safe in Christ Jesus, the Holy Spirit would freely send me places to give a word to someone God wanted to get a message to.

I was talking to two couples that were in the military, engaged with assignments. I reached out to them both about what God revealed to me for their spiritual walk. To share the word of God, the Holy Spirit gave me instructions to first give His word and then give them each some blessed oil. The first couple experienced a stillborn birth of a boy. I knew not this information before the Holy Spirit revealed the birth of two boys.

The Lord's word for them revealed they in fact would have two boys and be very happy. The last name of the first family was Abdulzahir. When I looked up the last name, it meant "Servant of the Manifest." I had blessed oil for each family. The second family I had seen were the Shields. I prayed for this family and blessed this family and gave them blessed oil. Their message from the Lord included a deeper love for one another. I was amazed at the Holy Spirit who added an additional family to give a message to. This family was added through God's servant. The last family I went to see were the Archers.

The head of the family was Michael Archer. My message from God was awesome. The Holy Ghost revealed a lot about this family to me, who had been under witchcraft and curses, which bound up their money and every move they made to move forward. I went with information the Holy Spirit gave me for them.

Each family trusted the word of God that was delivered. I hadn't realized I knew none of these families. I was in the airport calling my prayer partner, Shawna, sharing with her that I knew none of these families and they could cut me up and put me in their freezer. She laughed at me and said, "Disciple of God, go in the confidence that God got you covered." I felt tears coming down my face, not knowing why. The angels in the airport must have been happy to see me coming. I felt a little better after talking to Shawna.

For each family, I spent a day and was on a flight to my next destination, according to the Holy Spirit. I spent a total of six days giving the written word of God to each of the families, His Servant, His Shield, and His Archer.

These were the last names of each family the Holy Spirit had me to deliver a word from God and blessed oil to cover them. Several years later, I reached out to God's servants and learned they had two little boys. God's Shields are doing very well. God's Archers are doing very well too. They all welcomed me into their lives. The Holy Spirit downloaded information about them to me that only God and them knew. I said to God, "Here I am, Lord. Send me." And He did.

I never knew serving God was so interesting. What I thought was a mistake was actually a setup. It was explained to me that the rougher the journey, the bigger the blessing from God. God will expose the little distractions that keep you on one level and reveal challenges that stretch your understanding in faith in order to get you to a place where you are trusting Him more. My oldest daughter and her husband were stationed in New York, Watertown. My daughter had just had my first grandson.

Trusting Jesus to get us there, I made up in my mind that Jesus and I were going to see him. I asked Jesus to drive while I focused on His word and worshipped. I decided to go through Canada into New York. I had never driven that many miles before without someone in the car to drive with me. I had Jesus, and that was all I needed. Driving wasn't a problem; it was staying focused and not allowing distractions to take over. I brought with me several compact disks of my pastor's sermons. I also brought along the ride gospel music that was great.

I was driving in a straight lane highway in Canada, which allowed drivers to excel to seventy miles per hour versus fifty-five miles per hour. There was no one on the road except for me. I asked Jesus to drive because I got caught up in praise and worship from the sermon, which was very good.

I remember clapping my hands without holding on to the steering wheel for may be two to three minutes. Then it dawned on me that I did not have my hands on the steering wheel for a long time. I grabbed the wheel and started crying in amazement that it wasn't me driving all that time, but Jesus took the wheel and allowed me to worship. I was in awe all the way into New York. Before entering Canada, in Detroit, Michigan, there was construction going on.

I prayed to Jesus that He get me out of the maze and on the right track. Jesus had me follow sign after sign, I did not know if I was following the correct sign. I followed Jesus's instructions. When Jesus said turn right, I turned right, sign or no sign. When Jesus said turn left or right, I did just that. I didn't know where I was going or if I was going in the right direction, I trusted Jesus.

After about an hour, I saw signs that directed me to the correct highway that took me straight to my daughter's house. I was so excited to see them all. My grandson was a week old, and I was able to give him back to God as Hannah did her son, Prophet Samuel. This practice of giving every child born under my mantle/leadership back to God is a practice that is still done today. I made it back home in shorter time than it took me to arrive at my daughter's house.

I was awakened one night by an entity that was trying to cause my pressure to increase. I felt very bad and could feel the entity on me. I began to pray and call on Jesus for help. My body would be frozen, or I would feel something jump off my bed. I was never afraid. I knew as a believer I had power and God's angels with me.

I prayed that God would send His angels to protect around the inside and outside of my house and excel in strength and draw out their fiery swords (Psalm 103:20, KJV) to defeat any ungodly force.

During the summer about five years ago, God gave me a vision about angels covering the United States. The weather was strange that year. I prayed to God that He would send His warrior angels and position them around the perimeter of the United States. I saw in a vision mighty strong warrior angels positioned around the perimeter of the United States. They were tall, strong, and mighty with huge swords waiting to secure or to protect. Their wingspan was very vast. When their wings expanded, they touched the other warring angel's wings, strategically positioned with their backs toward the land.

That year, the entire United States experienced a heat wave that was so intense it made the history books because the heat went across *The United States* from the East Coast to the West Coast. I believe

God's warring angels are still in place protecting us because we are "One Nation Under God." I believe that is the reason we "*The United States*" have not had any major events due to angelic protection.

CHAPTER 6

GOD'S ANGELS

There have been many times I knew God's angels were present, and I knew I was safe. My prayer partner was speaking at church function. A she did not want to go by herself and asked me if I would go with her. I, of course, told her I would go. I would not have missed this event in her life for anything in the world. We met at church, and I rode with her to the other church location. The event was awesome. God really moved in her.

She spoke a word that was directly from God. She did not flinch or show weakness as she brought forth the word of God. After her delivery of the word we got back in the car. We talked about her performance and her word from God. I assured her she was great. We finally made it back to the church. We were sitting in her car, just talking. All of a sudden, I felt her car go down as though something huge sat on the top of her car. I asked her if she felt her car go down like something extremely huge sat on her car. She looked at me and said, "I did." We were not afraid at any cost, just amazed. We did not question the event as long as we both knew that God Almighty was protecting us.

I have known that God's angels were with me all of my life. From being a small girl, I could feel a tapping on my forehead in an attempt to be awakened in the morning to get ready for school to being pulled in the passenger seat of my car to avoid a head-on collision. When I tried to fight my battles, I had to go to God because they were too intense for me to handle, and God made a way for me to win (Exodus 14:14, KJV). Exodus 14:14 says, "The Lord shall fight for you, and you shall hold your peace."

I read that scripture and said, "The Lord shall fight my battles if I just hold my peace." I refuse to fight any issue that was bigger than me. When circumstances made me worry or experience feelings that brought doubt or fear, God came right away and made a way for me to escape.

I continued having visions of me fighting the enemy. I once had a dream of me being in the top box (skybox) at a football game. I like football and the team I cheered for. In this dream, the balcony booth turned into a place where there were many people, and I was a bystander that wanted to enjoy the football game.

Out of nowhere came a man in all black equipped with firing ammo that destroyed other men in black who were attempting to destroy. I remember they put me in the mind of a ninja. I wasn't afraid, but I thought I was watching a show from God. I woke up and tried to figure out what that dream was all about. I prayed and asked God about the meaning of the dream. I trusted God to protect me from whatever the dream, was protecting, those in the dream from. Soon, I forgot about the dream. I never had another dream that had men in black clothing (ninjas) or football games in them, I normally don't dream.

As time progressed and my thirst for God increased, I noticed, everything that I have ever asked God for He gave to me. When He began to stretch me in ways unfamiliar to me. I began to see my weaknesses through Him.

One summer day, I was lying on the floor by my patio door, enjoying the breeze coming into my house then I dozed off. I saw myself walking through a field leading to a park. I was trying to get to the other side for some reason.

At any rate, as I walked through the field, with every step the green grass cracked open, Gold coins bubbled up from the ground then I was amazed at the sight of seeing gold coins come out of the ground. I kept walking, and the same thing happened with every step. I had walked a long distance from where I had started.

I looked back and saw a trail of gold coins upon the top of the ground. I woke up after I looked back in awe at what God was trying to show me. Grateful at the vision, I thanked God for His love toward me. I called my prayer partner, Shawna, to see if God would give her insight to what the vision meant. Shawna had mentioned that there was a conference coming up in a nearby town. She suggested that we should attend the conference.

She had indicated that there was a young lady by the name of Debra who was a dreamer of dreams. A dreamer of dreams is a person whom God has endowed with the gift to interpret dreams or visions. I was so excited that I would meet someone in the body of Christ who could provide information to my vision. I asked my prayer partner if she trusted what she reveals in her interpretations from God. She said, "Yes." I did not know Debra, and I depended on Shawna to identify her for me.

After listening to the speakers, I wondered if she had attended the conference. My prayer partner assured me that Debra was in attendance. I never thought to ask God what the vision meant. The conference had ended, and we headed for the door. Debra never made her presence known. Then out of the blue a voice called out, "Shawna." My prayer partner looked in the direction of the call, and a smile came on her face. I decided that was Debra. Debra and I began to talk, and she educated me about dreams and visions that God gives His people.

She told me that God uses certain people, places, or things to reveal a message that is meant for you because those things are most relevant to the message He need you to see. Debra indicated that I must be highly favored in the heavenly realm because my vision meant that God has made earth to yield its treasures to me. It was good to hear the validation of what was given to me. I wondered what God had in store for me.

Debra indicated that I must have asked God for something that He was going to bestow to me. "He surely wanted to let you know because He made the vision very clear about His intentions. He wanted you to be in a mindset where he could secure your trust. Your destiny must be a great one."

Shawna gave to me a similar interpretation. I thanked Debra and went on my way to meet my prayer partner. On the way home, I shared what Debra told me. My prayer partner agreed with the interpretation given to me about the vision. I was very grateful in knowing God was leading me to where He needed me to be. Blessed be God!

In the King James Version, the Bible says in Proverbs 10:22, "The blessings of the Lord, it maketh rich, and HE addeth no sorrow with it." Also, Proverb 10:21 says, "The lips of the righteous feed many." The feeding many can be interpreted in many ways. I accept what God says in His Word about the Gospel, and I believe in God to keep his 7,487 promises.

I thought about the book of Proverbs when I started getting revelation about what God could do in my life. I got so happy. Proclaiming and believing the word of God and His son's works give the Holy Spirit the go-ahead to move in every area of your life is what I believe. His visions were just the beginning of God's gifts, and I had no clue what was coming next. I just trusted Jesus in whatever was on its way.

About a month later, I attended a woman's retreat at a location that fostered peaceful, serene environments. While on the retreat, I was pressed to show the gifting God gave me. Several ministers spoke a word to me. Most of them indicated who I was to God, and although I was always given a back seat to many in humility, God was going to make me first. I would be brought in the company of great men where I operated in the third heaven. I have been told these things before. I said like Mary, "Be it unto me."

While at the retreat, a member of our group misplaced her wedding ring. She began to freak out because she had just had it in her hand. The minister that was in our location said to me, "Where is it?" I looked at her like I had no idea what she was talking about because I did not have the young lady's ring. The minister said it again, and I saw in a vision that the ring was in a dark place on its side.

The young lady's ring was in a small place. After thirty minutes of looking in areas that could be small, there was a scream from an adjacent room from the young lady, she had found her ring. It was in a compartment in her purse where she said, "she had already taken everything out of her purse." The wedding ring was in the corner of her purse that she knew she had looked in and emptied out. My prayer partner has been my witness for thirteen-plus years to my supernatural events.

I was on my way to work on a Monday after the retreat. As I drove, I saw a vision that the moon and the planets moving in an elliptical motion in front of me right in the windshield of the car. I called my prayer partner, freaking out, because I could see them moving right in front of me.

Shawna said to me, "You are still in the spirit. Remain calm and pay attention to the road. Pull over if you have to." After forty-five minutes of riding, the vision began to disappear. I calmed down and was okay. I was in awe at what God wanted to reveal unto me by this vision. It was shared with me that God has given me greater gifts above the planets more than I knew of.

Visions are useful when God reassures you that He is greater than every situation that may come your way. One night, I was sleeping and saw myself in space. As I looked down, I could see the earth. Out of the abyss came fabric of purple, red, gold, and blue. Each fabric color began to wrap around me. I wasn't afraid as I felt the fabric on my person. I began to think about the visions God revealed to me over the weeks, months, and years. I am honored that God trusted me and loves me because of the visions and interpretations and what they meant. I received a Bible, which indicated the colors of God. This Bible indicated that the color of purple was of God, the color of red was of Jesus, the color of gold was of God, and the color of blue was of angels. The colors depicted colors of royalty. I wondered why the color of green wasn't in the colors of fabric. Green was the color of man.

My prayer partner, Shawna, and I would pray every morning at five. We were committed to pray in tongues for fifteen to twenty minutes daily. Sometimes the timeline would be extended to thirty minutes or so after being led by the Holy Ghost. We prayed in tongues because we wanted God to hear our petitions without anything interrupting our petitions. It was our way to touch and agree on what we were talking to God about.

Years ago, I used to play softball in my neighborhood. My team had won many awards for winning so many games. It was fun back then to compete, and it was just fun to meet other players. We had a championship game on the north side of town. We were scheduled to play the opposing team, and then coach was going to treat the team to pizza. I drove my car to the game. I would have never figured that I would end up in the hospital that day.

I remember hearing the acceleration of a car. The next thing I remember is a voice saying, "If it hit you, it will hurt," then I was snatched onto the passenger seat of my car. What happened was an oncoming driver had a seizure and collided into several cars including mine, head-on.

My softball coach had four of my team members in his car. I was in my car alone. The car hit with such force that the car in front of me flipped and slammed into my car. The driver ended up with his head on my window ledge. I remember the ambulance person coming to my car asking me if I was hurt. I thought I was all right. When I woke up, I was in the hospital ward of some type. I received a call from my momma telling me that my dad and her were on their way to take me home. The most disturbing thing was that I received calls from lawyers, and I did not even call them. I was told, by my sister, those lawyers were ambulance chasers.

I am so blessed. If the angel did warn me, that if the car hit me it would hurt me, I don't even think that I would be writing this book. The jerk on my shirt that put me into my passenger seat was real, and the man's head on my window seal was also real. I did not receive any major injuries like the other players. Their injuries extended to jaws being broken, ribs being broken, and legs being broken.

After two weeks, I went to visit those who received more severe injuries and had to make several doctors' visits. Most of all, God was on our side, no one expired. The accident event happened so fast it had to be the angels of God that saved each of our lives. The coach invited the team over for dinner to reflect on the accident and the game's sportsmanship displayed when the other team defeated us. It was a nice gesture, and it was the last time I saw any of them again. We just lost touch with one another due to most of us going off to college and life itself. That experience showed me just how fragile we as a people are, God's grace and mercy was on us all that day. Although we experience God's grace daily, we forget how He sends His angels to protect us from dangers that we never knew was coming our way. As I go from day-to-day thinking on how God's has empowered me to continue on my destiny in Him, I rest with ease in just knowing Jesus thought enough about me to include His angels to keep me, protect me, open doors for me, answer questions, and guide me along my journey. Blessed be God Almighty.

CHAPTER 7

JESUS STRONG

When I thought about what Jesus strong meant to me, I realized there was so much to share I could not do this on my own. I depend on Jesus to inform me on what events He wants me to share that would make a difference in someone's life. My journey into the kingdom of God is one that I believe all what the Bible says in regard to the promises left for me. I believe when Jesus said He would never leave me or forsake me (Hebrews 13:5, KJV), He would only send me places, were He had been there before me. Protection would be my covering, where anointing would be my right to perform the works that He had left for me to follow.

I meditate on the word of God, whether I receive it from my pastor or being led by the Holy Ghost. When Jesus and I talk, He provides answers to questions that I wondered about when it came to my Christian walk in Him. The atmosphere is peaceful in the Holy Spirit when learning how to understand life's journeys, which can be comforting. What I have learned from the Holy Spirit is the enemy only was sent to distract me so that I won't feel obligated in staying focused on what the Holy Spirit wanted to teach me. The Holy Spirit alerts me to evil environments in order to teach me strategy in overcoming attacks only God can defeat. I truly am humbled when I realize that the answers and actions that I take come directly from the Holy Spirit.

I worked two jobs one year. One job, I taught chemistry at a local college, and I worked the midnight shift at a local store. I would be so tired sometimes that the Holy Spirit would take over at any given time. The local store was where I worked midnights and experienced most spiritual events.

I was young in my faith on this level and did not have a clue as to why I would experience spiritual events. I would go to work and be assigned to put items on discount shelves. I would turn to answer a question, and when I would turn back around to continue loading the shelf, all of the items would be back into the cart. I wasn't afraid but not very happy that I had to restock the shelf again. Fear did not come into my heart. I believe Jesus protected me. Soon, I severed my relationship with that company. Many occurrences or events, which included evil interactions of torment, were won when Jesus sent His angels to fight for me.

When Jesus would fellowship with me, He would respond in a soft voice. Knowing the voice of God ensures the truth. The power of God is in the Word. In the Bible, Genesis 1:14 says, "And the word was made flesh and dwelled amongst us." Jesus is the manifested word of God being made flesh. Some of my experiences with truth involve the Holy Spirit. When I am experiencing offense, I have to redirect my concerns and emotions of displeasure toward the Word. Asking God to do something with my life meant that I am a product of Jesus. I know that He will never leave me nor forsake me (Hebrews 13:5, KJV). Just as I depend on Him to comfort, lead, guide, and keep safe my children and family, I am depending on Him to lead me through my tough times and enjoy the good times with me too.

Even though I have assignments in the physical world, Jesus has made sure that the truth is always in front of me in His word. When I am confronted with spiritual occurrences in the physical world, I call on Jesus, and I immediately remember: "Not by my power, nor by my might, but by the spirit of the Lord" (Zechariah 4:6, KJV). I am victorious. Hebrews 13:5 (KJV) says, "Let your conversation be without covetousness; and be content with such things as ye have: for He (Jesus) hast said, I will never leave you nor forsake you."

My family would come over, and we would enjoy talking about experiences in the Lord. We are all endowed with spiritual gifts from God. We share amazing testimonies about how good God is when we quote, "No weapon formed against us shall prosper and every tongue that rises up against us will be condemned for this is the heritage of the servants of the Lord and our righteousness is of the Lord" (Isaiah 54:17, KJV).

In arenas that are of a spiritual nature, I cannot tell unless things or normal day-to-day events seem strange. For example: I noticed that certain individuals who are normally a plus size are now slender in stature. Even if I take a second look at that individual, they will remain the same. At first, I was confused about what I was looking at, but the more I experienced this event, I began to realize that I was in the spirit. It is hard to determine whether you are in the spirit or in the physical realm.

The spiritual realm is not nice if you wear your feelings on your shoulder. The Holy Spirit will guide you through those moments of being in the spirit. Most of the time, individuals will seem to have a different demeanor from their usual posture on greeting and just being mean or being nice. Individuals rarely speak back or may seem to have an attitude about everything that is happening that day.

I have never been in the spirit for two days. Most times if I don't encounter an individual, I will not know if I am in the spirit. I do, however, realize that being in the spirit means that Jesus knows you can handle the information you are receiving.

Jesus is always watching to make sure that I know where I am going. Destiny is awesome when the Lord gives you an assignment. In relying on Jesus, I was training in another city for a job God had given me. I would come home every other weekend to pray and worship God. I would meet with a pastor and his sister. We went to a location where we could pray and worship to the Lord.

It seemed as though the Lord was right there with me. I trusted God to protect me each and every time I traveled to pray with them. I noticed that it appeared that the context of the visit was changing, and God removed me from their presence. I did not question the Lord's moving me from that environment. Years later that brother-sister combination began to spread untruths about me. I had no idea what lies they were telling. I trusted Jesus in protecting me and making all lies reveal the truth about what was on their agenda.

I forgave them in their attempts to lie about what was the true purpose of my visits to pray and worship because God sees all and knows all, Genesis 31:12, KJV. All that they tried to do, God took care of it. The Bible says, "No weapon form against me shall prosper" (Isaiah 54:17, KJV). I went to worship, and their plan was to make something out of nothing go on. I have moved on and let Jesus handle the issue. Even when I think back to my reasons for coming home was to pray and worship, I know He knows my heart.

I think about how miserable the world can be and how emotions can ride high when trusting the Lord is at the forefront of breaking through tough moments in life or when the Lord is blessing you when you don't know your next move. Most of my friends call that "The Great Setup." I love when Jesus takes control and you have no more concerns for fear isn't a factor anymore. Several years ago, I hit hardship and tried to sell my house to help remove some of the burden of losing my home. I made a promise to God that I just wanted to be set free from the mortgage without losing my home. Most people I knew did not have problems with losing their homes.

There were several offers on the house, but I did not keep my promise to the Lord. When I asked God for help, I told Him that I would not be greedy. I just wanted to get free from the obligation of the mortgage. The next buyers who came to see the house, I told the Lord I would sell it to them. It took a few more showings for the last couple asked me to sell them my house. The Lord made a way, and I did not lose my house but sold it!

Jesus was making changes in my life, and I did not know that I had to walk it out. I could not get out of that process in moving forward and my success in the Lord's will from my life and destiny.

The more I found myself in trouble through life's journey for choosing the Lord, the more I could not understand why I was going through this type of treatment. I had to see what I couldn't see. Looking in the spirit by my inner man allowed me to envision what was going on in my life, and where I was going would be greater than where I came from. I figured Jesus had all the answers.

I was drawn to certain preachers that would deliver a word from God that would set me back on solid ground. I was hurting inside so bad about not having the finer things in life; it bothered me especially because I was a child of the Most High God. Although I did not lose my home, I sold it; I realized I was homeless. I was a real estate agent. This made it easier to sell my own home, but for the other homes that were sold, the devil had the owners of the real estate company keep my commission. I never got paid for the sale of two homes I sold. I had to let it go because I felt hopeless knowing there were no laws that governed that area. I gave it to God.

I called on Jesus so much I wanted more of God than ever before. I knew I was in the school of the Holy Ghost because I experienced events that did not bother me. When I would go to church, it seemed that my spirit would be at peace. I would immediately feel the peace of God. Even today, I travel and attend church, not only to hear the Word, but also to rest in the atmosphere of the Holy Spirit.

When I read Smith Wigglesworth's book on the Holy Spirit, I experienced the truth about my power in being a believer that Jesus left in us being guided by God's mighty spirit. I would chew on bits and pieces of Smith Wigglesworth's book because I wanted to digest each meaningful word in its pure form as the Holy Ghost brought meaning to Wigglesworth's experiences. That very power that Jesus left for us is real. Most of the time I would have a pain that I did not have before. I figured it must be someone who was experiencing pain in that area.

First, I would pray for everyone whom the Lord would bring to mind who might have that kind of pain. Sometimes the Holy Spirit would give me a specific name like Karen, Tom, Timothy, Marci, or Byron. The Holy Spirit would tell me to pray for men, women, and children that might be experiencing that kind of pain advancing inside of them. Then after praying for them, I would tell that pain to leave my body, and it would walk out of the area it was in my body.

The entity was a separate thing, and the moment I spoke to it, I could feel it leave my body. This was always the case. It is the power and works of Jesus through the Holy Spirit in me. When I moved into my house, it was very beautiful and had very little work to be done to it. I was excited about how good God was to send me this house. Little did I know that there was something that wasn't quite right with it. There was a black light in the middle of the living room. I wondered what was going on. The previous owner must had been involved in something, and I just did not know what. The Holy Ghost is awesome. I knew I was protected by God, and fear would try to appear every now and then to divert my thoughts and emotions.

God does not make mistakes when He sends His elect into battle. My angels and the wisdom of God stay posted in front of me. I learned in my reading that evil can only go as far as you allow it to. Our power lies in Christ Jesus, and it is through Christ that we are strong, blessed, empowered, healed, delivered, set free, dwell in safety, favored, and strong in the power of His might. In the Bible, Psalms 5:12 (KJV) says, "For thou, Lord, will bless the righteous; with favor wilt thou compass him as with a shield."

First John 5:14–15 (KJV) says, "And this is the confidence that we have in him, that, if we ask any thing according to his will, he hearth us: And if we know that he hears us, whatsoever we ask, we know that we have the petitions that we desired of Him." Jesus continues to increase my faith being the word of God and in His works since the word was made flesh; and the spirit of God moves as the power of God.

CHAPTER 8

$\bullet \blacklozenge \blacklozenge \blacklozenge \blacklozenge \bullet$

HOLY SPIRIT

When I became acquainted with the Holy Spirit, I read that He was sent by God to comfort us once Jesus returned to heaven. The Holy Spirit sometimes referred to as the Holy Ghost has made Christian life easy when the Bible is the model, reference, and guide in living life in Christ Jesus. I have witnessed the power of the Holy Ghost move upon situations that seemed impossible. I have been the recipient of the protection of the Holy Ghost moving to the turn of being in places that I had no idea why I was there until I had seen a person and all of the dots connected. The Holy Spirit began to download information that that person needed to hear to be in a certain place, make a certain decision, or perform a certain task.

I had decided not to go to church one Saturday. I wanted to spend time alone reading the Bible and enjoying the quiet time. At the last minute, I had the urge to go to church. I hadn't realized that church would conclude about fifteen minutes after I had arrived. I really didn't care about being extremely late. My mind wasn't on anyone in particular. I figured the Lord would let me know whom I was there for. The moment I arrived at church, I saw a young lady whom I knew from new members class. She looked like she was in need of some answers. She saw me come into the building and into the sanctuary. When we shared a smile, I knew immediately that she was the person God wanted me to deliver a message to.

While I was at home, I made dinner for my family. I made extra just in case someone brought a guest home (one of their friends). I stopped and chatted for a minute, and then I shared with her that I would not have come to church if the Lord had not sent me. I told Nikki that I had no clue of the person I was supposed to meet until I saw her. The conversation went on for about a half hour. She shared that she had some difficult decisions to make about her family, relocating, and her new job.

I shared with Nikki what God had given me to share with her concerning what He had for her. She was happy that the pressure she was under had been relieved. She also stayed the night and indicated that my house was peaceful. I told her I had so many of God's angels in my house that it was funny. I thanked her for saying so because I thought it a privilege to have someone come into my home and feel the presence of the Lord.

Morning came. She had left before we could say goodbye. She indicated that she had a drive to make, and she promised to visit again. That was over fifteen years ago. She is doing fine and has a little boy. When I hear the Holy Spirit, I am guided to be still or to move in a certain direction.

When, I got a position for a job I applied for, I had to train in a city that was five hours away from my home. I really did not mind, but I really missed my family. Traveling between home and training was not so bad. I would come home to pray and worship. After being home over the weekend, it was time to go back to my training location. I was traveling seventy-five miles per hour and did not realize that something was going on up ahead of me. About a half mile ahead, there was a crazy rainstorm. I did not know there was a rainstorm ahead of me. All of a sudden, my vehicle began to slow down and jerk as though someone was pressing on my breaks.

I understood at that moment that I needed to slow down because I was going too fast. About five minutes of slowing down, there it was! There was a rainstorm right in front of me! It was raining so hard I could not see the vehicle right in front of me. Traffic came to a standstill, and many of the vehicles pulled off to the side of the road due to poor visibility. If I had not slowed down and went into that rainstorm at seventy-five miles per hour, I would not be writing to you.

I trust in the spirit of the Lord. I do not ask questions when I am being led. I also do not inquire about things I am supposed to say. I just open my mouth, and the Lord fills my mouth with what is supposed to be said, Psalms 81:10, KJV. Sometimes, I pay attention even to what I am saying because I know that it is not me conveying the wisdom that I hear coming out of my mouth.

Most times when the Holy Spirit takes over, I am in awe at what I am being taught. I feel empowered by knowing that I am covered. I take nothing for granted when I know that the Holy Spirit is moving on my behalf. I watched a movie the other day, and the main character was a gentle man that had the highest clearance in the world for the skills he had possessed. This character was labeled "The Equalizer." As I watched the movie, this character went into territories that were extremely ruthless because of the cartels that ran the organizations. The Equalizer did not show any mercy unto the bad guys who were very mean and had no regard about human life. They (the bad guys) preyed on the weak, and if anyone crossed them or betrayed them, they had no mercy on them.

The Equalizer, however, took great concern for those people who could not defend themselves or victims because they were in the wrong place at the wrong time. He moved with calculated precision without a mistake being made when engaging with the bad guys. The bad guys were confident that they could overtake him because he was alone. He took a moment to envision each move based on the position of the bad guy. Within seconds, the room was quiet with every bad guy being exterminated. He cut down the root of the problem. His demeanor was humble and meek. He was willing to help those who could not help themselves because of the resources they didn't have.

I asked God why was I watching this movie. I am a science-medical type of girl. Fairness is a big issue that I try to maintain along with being transparent in my actions. I began to think about the Holy Spirit who has the highest clearance in the universe, who God Himself sent to protect us, lead and guide us, to empower us, and to make sure that the word of God stays tried and true for God's people. The Holy Spirit is the equalizer for the children of God. The Holy Spirit fights for all of God's children against all of our enemies. The Holy Spirit has connections that allow us to move in protection. The Holy Spirit equalizes our destinies that have been ordained by God. The Holy Spirit cut down the unseen enemy in such a way they are never seen again. The Holy Spirit sees every angle, every possibility, every outcome, and every victory. The Holy Spirit is swift and more accurate than we could ever imagine, John 14:15-31, KJV.

The Holy Spirit brings hope to a situation that would not be possible, if God had not sent him. The Holy Spirit brings peace of mind as Jesus assures us that He will never leave us nor forsake us. Just know that in all things, the Holy Spirit is there to make sure that the children of God have an equal chance and the victory is ours. I watched the equalizer take out all of the bad guys from the top person to all of his so-called enforcers. I felt confident, and my faith increased, and peace was restored in watching this movie. When I am led to watch a movie, I get curious as to why I am watching this type of movie. Most often, a connection is made, and I take note of the outcome of the movie.

The confidence is in knowing that the battle is not mine—it's the Lord's (2 Chronicles 20:15, KJV). This assurance comes with benefits from God that as long as your faith and belief in God's word, His son's (Jesus) work and in the Holy Spirit's assignment in our lives, we will overcome as long as we learn and walk out the journey trusting in God.

CHAPTER 9

WARFARE: IT'S REAL

When I thought about the spiritual realm, I mediated on what I would see. Would I see the many entities moving around without limit? I had to ask God what the unseen was like. The Lord answered my question. The movie *Constantine* came out in the 1990s. When it did, I believe it was because I asked God, "What was the unseen realm really like?" The movie engaged my thoughts when the many spiritual occurrences took place involving the main character who had lived through many experiences wanted to expire to end his assignment.

Regardless of the experience to fight off the ungodly beings tormenting humans, Constantine (fought them off and sent them back to hell) would come to capture the ungodly beings in a manner only his skills and experience could defeat. Constantine had experience as a demon slayer. It did not matter to him if the entity was of any level; he would go after it like it was his job to do so. Fear wasn't a factor when it came to engaging them. He had no worries but confidence in God watching what he was doing and ultimately his victory in combat.

Now as it pertained to the Bible, God has sent His Holy Spirit, archangels, warring angels, guardian angels, angelic host, and ministering angels to combat all of the circumstances in which God's people needed help. I am grateful God sees everything and has been everywhere that we have been, even before we have walked the ground. As He did with Moses, giving him the ground, he walked on (Joshua 1:3, KJV).

Realizing my power and authority as a believer are strengthened by the Holy Spirit to send ungodly entities to the lake of fire or a dry and desolate place in the name of Jesus increased my faith. Being a child of the Most High God was the power Jesus left for me in the Holy Spirit.

I had traveled to Hawaii to see my daughter who had just had my grandson. He was about two weeks old when I arrived at their house, and I was excited to be there with them. My son-in-law was in Afghanistan because of him being in the army. My daughter was stressed because the baby was in the hospital due to asthmatic symptoms. This was their second son.

When I arrived, I met my daughter at the hospital. My husband came over to help with our first born grandson. We were in the hospital about three days, and during that time, cultures were taken that would give an indication of what my grandson had that put him in the hospital. Outside of being short of breath, he was just two weeks old. The cultures had not come back yet, and the doctors wanted to take fluid from his spine.

What did not make sense was that the cultures they had taken had not come back yet. I called my church and asked for an elder. The Bible says in James 5:14 (KJV), "Is anyone among you sick? Let him call for the elders of the church and let them pray over him anointing him with oil in the name of the Lord; and the prayer of faith shall save the sick and the Lord shall rise him up." The church elder on duty indicated that they would not normally be in attendance at the church, and it must be meant for us to pray for my grandson as we agreed on his healing. As my husband arrived, I called my daughter who informed me that the X-ray indicated over a 75 percent improvement. Blessed be God Almighty!

This was music to my ears. I picked up my husband, and we took our other grandson home to stay with him. In the house, I noticed my grandson as he walked passed by me, he grinned in such a way evil reeked from his demeanor. Before I knew it, I had grabbed that entity out of my grandson. I also knew I had him in my hand.

I could hear it beg for me to send it to a dry and desolate place verses into the lake of fire. I was not playing around with anything I couldn't see, Jesus Christ certainly didn't. It was a new experience for me now that I think about the event.

I followed Jesus's foundation (His works) when it came to handling unseen entities. I sent it to a dry and desolate place knowing that it could not ever be removed from that place, in the name of Jesus. Since the day had been a long one after feeding my grandson, I knew he was sleepy. The moment the demon was removed from him, he fell so hard on the pillow asleep, I knew he was resting.

Over the years I have experienced teachings while being in the school of the Holy Spirit. Being in the school of the Holy Spirit is like taking a specialized course in learning stuff that only could be taught by God. For example: what you learn being in the school of the Holy Spirit is about your surroundings and how to not care about the stuff you have given to God. The cares that burden you are no longer your concern but that of the Lord (2 Corinthians 10:5, KJV). I have learned how to discern when an ungodly entity tries to engage my thoughts to pull me in, in order to distract me. I have learned to speak the word of God only for all situations that involve my emotions or thoughts, even in my mind. I take every thought captive and bring it under the Lord. It does not matter if it is a good thought or bad thought.

The Holy Spirit empowers me to defeat the enemy on a spiritual level. I move in fasting holistically—holistically in the manner that Moses did by being covered by God Almighty. When Moses went up the mount to spend time with God, Moses fasted and God gave him the bread of life and sustained him by giving Moses the living water (John 6:35, 7:37-38, KJV). This philosophy I use when I am fasting in accordance with the instructions I receive from the Holy Spirit. I want God to take His time in guiding me, in downloading information, wisdom, understanding, hearing His instructions on matters to come, inventions, visions, and in abilities to think past certain concerns that only God can correct as well as speaking in tongues as my communication during my period of fasting.

It is always for increase in knowledge of the ways of God and how He wants me to move in peace by allowing Him to take over. At first, it is not an easy thing to surrender control over as it pertains to your entire life. It does, however, over time become easier to let God have His way as you defeat the enemy at His own game by using God's methods for His kingdom in peace and living.

Spiritual warfare is real, but victory in every situation is real as well. God is faithful and will deliver you every time if you allow Him as Exodus 14:14 says, "God will fight your battles, if you just hold your peace." There will be battles that will be won that you had no knowledge of. Most individuals really want to fight the battle on their own, not realizing that they can't fight what they can't see. Only God can provide the knowledge in how to stay victorious while engaged in spiritual battles. The lead for any battle is the Holy Spirit and the living word of God (Jesus Christ).

Once the enemy realizes that you have employed the Word and work of God in every situation, then you will find that your experiences in spiritual warfare are engaged by the Holy Spirit because you understood that the battle was not yours; it's the Lord's (2 Chronicles 20:15, KJV). When my situations got difficult and I could not see my way through, I remembered that in the Bible, Hebrews 4:12 says, "For the word of God is quick, and powerful, and sharper than any two edged sword, piercing even to the dividing asunder of soul and spirit, and of the joints and marrow, and is a discerner of the thoughts and the intents of the heart."

To me, that meant what evil had in store for me as a devise of distraction or hurt my God had already made preparations for my victory. This gave me at peace and restored my faith in trusting Jesus with all my battles, concerns, protection, health, victories, and favor.

Having the authority to act in the way of speaking to a *thing* in the name of Jesus tested my faith when I meant business. Jesus did not entertain any evil force that had inhabited His people. In the book of Acts (19:14–17, KJV), a story of seven sons of Sceva (priest) who heard Paul had cast out devils in a person motivated them to try to repeat this event. When they thought they could perform this event the seven sons of this Sceva (priest) ran into the streets and found a person who was occupied by a devil and commanded that thing to come out of him. To their surprise the evil entity answered and said, "Jesus I know, and Paul I know, but who are you? And the man in whom the evil spirit was in leaped on them, and overcame them, and prevailed against them, so that they fled out of that house naked and wounded.

And this was known to all the Jews and Greeks also dwelling at Ephesus, and fear fell on them all, and the name of the Lord Jesus was magnified."

The sons of the Sceva (priest) a Jew did not have the heart of God in them. God gives protection to us, His children and by no means shall anything hurt us. We are His people, and He is our God (Jeremiah 30:22, Hebrew 8:10, KJV).

CHAPTER 10

◆◆◆◆◆

ONLY GOD

When I think about all of the supernatural events that have happened in my life, I think about the Bible scriptures that I have stood on to make it through. After reading the Bible, I remember scriptures that came alive in my life. Psalm 5:12 says, "For thou, Lord, wilt bless the righteous; with favor wilt thou compass him as with a shield." I use the Bible scriptures to keep me on track with daily battles. Exodus 14:14 says, "God will fight my battles if I just hold my peace." It took me a long time to understand that it wasn't about me fighting the battle but allowing God to fight my battles in every area of my life. When God manifested His goodness in my life, my whole life changed. It seemed like I looked out a new pair of lenses, and my thinking about issues that kept me distracted eventually disappeared.

I went on a business trip to learn more about my area of interest in the job I performed. I had not realized that I was taking too many milligrams in vitamins, or so I thought. Although the vitamins were good for me, I thought I was taking them too frequently. I also thought my body became toxic due to the amount of elemental supplement. For example: I was taking iron in low dose increments. I would take them every other day and did not think to spread them out over a couple of weeks versus every other day. So sitting in my hotel room, I felt like my mind and body was suffering from an attack of some sort. I tried to handle this issue on my own. When

I took the vitamins, I felt better for only a few minutes. It was five in the morning, and I could not sleep. I knew that what I was going through was a spiritual attack I did not know what to do.

I called a friend. Knowing that she would probably be asleep and not answer the phone did not stop me because it was the lifeline I needed to fight off what was tormenting me. When Evetta, a mighty woman of God, answered, I began to cry because God had sent me someone who would minister the word of God to me. I explained to her my issues. She told me that God would not allow anything to hurt me. We talked for hours it seemed. Evetta said she would cover me until I made it home. The Holy Spirit led me to get some tea. The moment I sipped the brew of tea, I felt a peace from the inside out. Psalm 3 (KJV) in the Bible tells of the Lord protecting His people.

I began to wonder why I was experiencing this type of attack. I began to realize that whatever was happening with me was why I was being attacked. I had confidence in the Lord allowing things to happen in order for me to become stronger in the area that I professed as my ministry. Throughout the Bible, Jesus treated evil spirits with a "no tolerance" demeanor. Jesus reversed the curses of those who lacked knowledge in spiritual warfare. Jesus did not allow the evil spirits to speak and He cast them out.

Slowly, the Holy Spirit began to instruct me in learning to overcome the demonic attacks. I had to read the Bible and learn of my authority as a believer. I joined a new church and brought compact discs to listen to while I was in my car. The Lord never left me alone. I began to understand my environment and was committed to do learning about warfare. I prayed to God that I wanted more of Him. I asked the Lord to use my life.

As time went on, I learned that I was being attacked by demonic forces. The Holy Spirit guided me in learning about my rights and authority left to me by Jesus Christ. I had not realized that I was being controlled and needed for God to come in and guide me through the power I had in Him. I needed to see what I could not see. In the Bible, Ephesians 1:18 says, "The eyes of your understanding being enlightened." I really needed for my eyes to be opened so I could see what I could not see. Oh, how I prayed every night that God would give me more of Him. I noticed that God had begun to lead me toward overcoming the entities that were attacking me. I learned that the area in which I moved was infested with evil.

I would have crazy mail, stupid text messages, and mean people trying to discourage me from my goals. I put in many applications for jobs that I knew that I could perform and was not hired. I actually got a job and was never called. Jesus never let me down. I began to get better in my thinking and in my physical body. I saw things that happened, and I wasn't afraid of them. Sitting at home, I would say out loud that Jesus was my exorcist, and the hallway light cover fell from the ceiling. That did not bother me either. I knew at that time that Jesus started a shift in the battle. My confidence was in Jesus and He sees everything (Genesis 31:12, KJV).

Second Kings 6:17 says, "And Elisha prayed, and said, Lord, I pray thee, open his eyes, that he may see. And the Lord opened the eyes of the young man and he saw and behold, the mountain was full of horses and chariots of fire around Elisha." I knew as my eyes began to open when I saw the truth.

I had given the enemy too much power. I began to trust Jesus more and took my power back from the enemy. I move in Christ Jesus. My protection, my peace, my joy, my health, my power, and my love are all through Jesus Christ. I have only just begun to share phenomenal favor, inventions, and conversations with the Lord. Great is His faithfulness. In the Bible, Psalms 62:5 says, "I depend on God alone." God is my only source. In the Bible, Malachi 3:10–11 reassures me that in focusing on God being my only source, He would keep me as I sow seeds of faith toward any mountain in my life, finances, personage, and family. In Jesus's name.

I had a question that only God could reveal to me. That question was how much more would He bestow to me?

ABOUT THE AUTHOR

Dr. Soretta Patton is one of five children born to parents that promoted their children in their goals and education. Soretta is the owner and managing broker for a Christian based company. Soretta has four children and many grandchildren. Believing in the bible, Soretta will tell you that God gets all the glory for everything that has been bestowed and given to her through grace.

CPSIA information can be obtained
at www.ICGtesting.com
Printed in the USA
BVHW031409310321
603653BV00013B/1071